It was a sunny day in the middle of Summer. There were buttercups, poppies, daisies and clover in the fields next to the wood.

A little rabbit was chewing the grass among the flowers. She was grey and white. She was called Silver.

BANG! There was a gunshot.

Silver ran to the hedge for cover. She hid under the leaves and branches. She shivered. She was frightened.

BANG! There was another gunshot. Silver stayed still for a moment. Then she ran out of her shelter and into the middle of the field. BANG! BANG!

Silver ran over the daisies and the clover as fast as she could. She dived under the hedge at the other side of the field.

Thump ... thump ... thump. Her heart was thumping. Silver was frightened. She hid under the cover of the leaves and branches.

Silver stayed still for a few moments. Everything was quiet. Her heart stopped thumping. Now she had to get back to her burrow in the wood.

So she hopped along the edge of the field. No one saw her. There were no more gunshots. Soon she came to the wood.

Her burrow was under an old oak tree. She ran to it as fast as she could. She dived into her underground home.

At last she was safe in her burrow. No one would find her there. She felt better. She lay down and she went to sleep.

"er"

Summer	cover
flowers	under
clover	her
Silver	over
buttercups	were
underground	other
better	another
shivered	shelter